CNN Student News
for Reading & Writing

Fuyuhiko Sekido
•
Jake Arnold
•
Ken Ikeda
•
Masato Kogure

Asahi Press

《《《 音声ストリーミング・ダウンロード配信 》》》

http://text.asahipress.com/free/english/

この教科書の音声は、
上記ウェブサイトにて無料で配信しています。

CNN Student News for Reading & Writing
Copyright © 2019 by Asahi Press

All rights reserved. No part of this book may be reproduced or transmitted in any form or by any means, electronic or mechanical, including photocopying, recording or by any information storage and retrieval system, without permission in writing from authors and the publisher.

はしがき

　このテキストはアメリカの学生向けニュース番組CNN Student News（現在はCNN 10）を用いて日本の学習者、主に大学生のみなさんが英語のリーディング力、ライティング力をつけやすいように編集、執筆されたテキストです。実際の番組は毎回約10分間、土日を除くほぼ毎日放送され、WEB上でも更新、配信されています。本テキストではそれらの中から約2～3分で完結しているニュースを選び教材化しました。内容は執筆者たちがバラエティに富むようにと心がけ、様々なジャンルから選んでいます。また、英語自体も難しくなりすぎていないものを選んだので、英語があまり得意でない方たちでも学ぶことができるように努めました。Unitは全部で15 Unitsあるので、担当の先生の方針によっては1回の授業に1 Unitで半期に、あるいは2回の授業に1 Unitを用いて通年で、学んでいく可能性がありますが、その指示に従って学習していってください。

　各Unitは、内容は違うものの、学習していく順序や項目は同じ構成になっています。まずニュースに関する概要をIntroductionで読みます。その後実際に放送された映像を見てスクリプトを読み、内容を確認しながら練習問題を解きニュースのテーマを理解します。その後、ニュースに出てきた単語に関する練習問題を解き、単語の理解を深めます。最後に、同じくニュースに出てきた単語を用いて要約を書いてみます。このように様々な種類の問題を用意してありますので、予習・復習などを含めて先生の指示に従っていろいろな側面、やり方で学んでいけることでしょう。また、別途用意してあります音声は、放送そのままのオリジナル放送音源と、それをスタジオでゆっくりとしたスピードで読み直したスロースピード音源の2種類を用意してありますので、生のニュースを聴き取る練習もできます。

　なお、本テキストの各Unitは既刊のCNN Student News vol. 1～5で扱ったUnitから好評だったものを選び、新たなスタイルに再編しました。このテキストを通してみなさんがCNN Student News（CNN 10）に関心を持ち、楽しみながら学習していけることを願っています。

　本テキスト執筆にあたり、朝日出版社の朝日英一郎様を始め、スタッフの方々に多大なるご支援、ご協力をいただきました。また、執筆協力として田所メアリーさん、長和重先生からは鋭いご指摘、ご助言を賜りました。この場を借りて、御礼申し上げます。

著者一同

Contents

Unit 1 Can Babies Choose Between Good and Bad? 1

Unit 2 Half-Empty or Half-Full? 5

Unit 3 How to Pass a Test 9

Unit 4 Soccer Brain Study 13

Unit 5 Google Glass for Firefighters 17

Unit 6 Women on Submarine 21

Unit 7 iPhone Musician 25

Unit 8 Bringing People Back to Baseball 29

Unit 9 Smell of Success 33

Unit 10 Octocopter 37

Unit 11 Staying Safe Online 41

Unit 12 Air Pollution in Asian Cities 45

Unit 13 Protecting Michelangelo's Paintings 49

Unit 14 Choosing Jury 53

Unit 15 Light Pollution 57

Unit 1

Can Babies Choose Between Good and Bad?

Reading

This is an introduction to the news.

We know that babies, three to six months old, are able to smile and cry to show their emotions, but until recently it was thought that they had no sense of what is right and wrong. Scientists at Harvard, however, have carried out a study which seems to suggest that this is not true.

In the study, babies watch a puppet show in which they are shown bunny rabbit characters. There is a green bunny who is kind and helpful and an orange bunny who is mean. After the show, the babies can choose one of the bunnies, and most of the babies choose the green bunny, the good one. This shows that the children prefer good characters to bad ones.

In the next part of the study, the bunnies are holding snacks: graham crackers. The good bunny has one, and the bad bunny has two. Again, most of the babies will take a cracker from the good bunny, even though that bunny has fewer crackers. However, if the bad bunny has eight crackers and the good bunny only one, the babies are more likely to take a cracker from the bad bunny, suggesting that there is a limit to this moral sense.

Try this

After reading the text above, close your textbook and in 30 seconds summarize the content to your partner. You can use Japanese or English.

Transcript Completion

Watch the news clip.

AZUZ: If you've spent any time around babies, so we are talking children three to six months in age, you know they can express themselves. Smiling when happy, crying when — well, whenever. But do they know right from wrong? Good from bad? Do babies have a sense of morality? A scientist at Yale University says psychologists have long felt that babies knew nothing in that area. One study is changing that, but there is a caveat.

REPORTER: These babies at Yale University's Infant Cognition Center are here to watch a puppet show. A show designed to illustrate examples of good and bad behavior. Watch as this puppet struggles to open a box. A green bunny comes along and helps to open the box. Green bunny is nice and helpful. Then, an orange bunny comes along and slams the box shut. The orange bunny is mean, unhelpful. But what does this mean to six-month-old and three-month-old babies? After repeated shows, they are presented with two puppets, the nice green bunny and the mean orange bunny. Which one will they choose?

Over 80 percent of babies like the nice puppet. So we see babies recognizing good and bad characters. But do they then try to avoid the bad guy? The good bunny has one graham cracker, the bad bunny has two. Which one will the babies choose? Over 80 percent of babies will take one cracker from the nice guy, avoiding the mean guy, even though he has one more cracker.

But what if the mean guy has eight crackers, and the nice guy just one cracker? Now, which one will the baby choose? 65 percent of babies will take the crackers from the mean guy. According to the study, more crackers means more willingness to overlook dealing with the bad guy.

CNN Student News – 2014

Unit 1

Comprehension Questions

Mark the following sentences True (T) or False (F). Underline the key words or phrases in the transcript which support your answer.

Paragraph 1

[T / F] (1) Azuz thinks that babies can express themselves.
[T / F] (2) A new study says that babies always know the right thing.

Paragraph 2

[T / F] (3) The babies go to the university to help with a puppet show.
[T / F] (4) The orange bunny does not help open the box.

Paragraph 3

[T / F] (5) The good bunny is given more crackers than the bad one.
[T / F] (6) Babies always prefer the bunny with more crackers.

Paragraph 4

[T / F] (7) The babies sometimes choose the good bunny with one cracker.
[T / F] (8) The babies' judgment is affected by both morality and crackers.

Notes:

caveat: 補足説明 / **Infant Cognition Center:** 乳児知覚センター / **bunny:** ウサギ / **slam:** バタンと閉める / **graham cracker:** 全麦粉クラッカー

Writing I

Select the best choice to complete the sentence.

1. He (　　　) how to go to the park with maps and gestures.
   - **a.** illustrate **b.** illustrated **c.** illustrating **d.** illustration

2. When my father refused to let me go, I told him he was being (　　　).
   - **a.** mean **b.** means **c.** meant **d.** meaning

Writing II

Select the best choice to complete the sentence.

1. It's good business and good (　　　) to save the environment.
2. That teacher uses (　　　) to teach grammar to her class.

   struggled / puppets / willingness / psychologist / overlooks / morality

Writing III

Write a summary of the news using the four words which are the correct answers to Writing I and Writing II above. Underline each of the four words.

Unit 2

Half-Empty or Half-Full?

Reading

This is an introduction to the news.

Do you want to be happy? Of course, you do! It is natural to want to be happy. However, it can be difficult to find happiness because we do not know what it is. Do we become happy because we have many of the best things? Or because we are successful in our study or our work? Our clip today looks at one thing that we know changes our chances of being happy: the way we think.

If we think that we have many friends and feel connected to the society we live in, there is more chance that we will be happy and have a longer life. A feeling of good social connection actually changes our bodies so that we can have a longer life. If we want to be happier for longer, we should try to make good connections with other people.

Being optimistic or pessimistic, positive or negative in our thinking, can also affect our happiness. Research has shown that if we think positively, we can be happier and live healthier and longer lives. If we think negatively, then we are more likely to be unhappy and become sick. Even if you do not feel positive, you should try to be optimistic so that you can be happy!

Try this

After reading the text above, close your textbook and in 30 seconds summarize the content to your partner. You can use Japanese or English.

Transcript Completion

Watch the news clip.

AZUZ: All right, besides getting on "Roll Call", what would make you happy? A new phone, money, an A in this class? There's nothing about happiness in the U.S. Constitution, but there is in the Declaration of Independence ... that one of our certain unalienable rights is the pursuit of happiness. It seems, to some extent, how happy and positive we are starts with our mindset.

UNIDENTIFIED MALE: Happiness isn't just a pleasant thing you feel. Science proves it's much deeper than that. Feeling happy actually helps you live a longer, healthier life. But how? For a large part, our happiness is tied to our social connections. In fact, if you don't have at least one close friend, you are less likely to be happy. Each of us has these things called telomeres. Those are tiny caps on our DNA chromosomes, that measure our cellular age. And it turns out, they also measure how many friends we have. No friends equals shorter telomeres. So by simply being social, you can actually slow down your biological age, living longer and happier.

Time for a pop quiz. Is this glass half-empty or half-full? If you said half-full, you are on your way to feeling happier and healthier. A Harvard study found that optimists are 50 percent less likely to have heart disease or a heart attack or a stroke. Keeping an overall optimistic attitude actually offers protection against cardiovascular disease.

Science doesn't fare as well for pessimists. They not only have lower levels of happiness compared to optimists, but research shows that people with negative thoughts are three times as likely to develop health problems as they age. So, what do you do if you are not a naturally happy person? Well, experts say the key is to act as though you are an optimist, even if you are not.

CNN Student News – 2014

Comprehension Questions

Mark the following sentences True (T) or False (F). Underline the key words or phrases in the transcript which support your answer.

Paragraph 1

[T / F] (1) Both the Declaration of Independence and the U.S. Constitution talk about happiness.

[T / F] (2) Our mindset decides completely how happy we are.

Paragraph 2

[T / F] (3) Feeling happy will help you live longer.

[T / F] (4) Having close friends makes us happier.

Paragraph 3

[T / F] (5) Optimists have more chance of good health and happiness.

[T / F] (6) If you say the glass is half-full, your chance of a heart attack increases.

Paragraph 4

[T / F] (7) Optimists are often less happy than pessimists.

[T / F] (8) Pessimists who act like optimists will be healthier.

Notes:

Roll Call: 出席確認 (番組内の短い高校紹介コーナー) / **Declaration of Independence:** 独立宣言 / **unalienable right:** 奪われてはいけない権利 / **to some extent:** ある程度 / **DNA chromosome:** DNA 染色体 / **cellular age:** 細胞年齢 / **and it turns out:** つまりは / **telomere:** テロメア (染色体末端部位) / **cardiovascular:** 心循環系の / **fare well:** 味方する

Writing I

Select the best choice to complete the sentence.

1. She's such an (　　　). She always looks for the positive.
   - a. optimist　b. optimists　c. optimistic　d. optimistically

2. He is very cheerful, so it is (　　　) to be with him.
   - a. please　b. pleasure　c. pleasant　d. pleasantly

Writing II

Select the best choice to complete the sentence.

1. Don't be such a (　　　)! Everything is going to be alright!

2. He has a strong (　　　), so he doesn't panic easily.

   key / pessimist / pursuit / mindset / stroke

Writing III

Write a summary of the news using the four words which are the correct answers to Writing I and Writing II above. Underline each of the four words.

Unit 3

How to Pass a Test

Reading

This is an introduction to the news.

Most people do not like testing at school. If you are taking a very important test, like the SAT test, or any other kind of test, today's clip gives some advice about what to do to get ready for and then to take a test.

Sleep well before the test. Eight hours is best, but if you can not get that much, then try to get as much as you can. If you do not sleep well, you will not be able to focus on the test. Remember to set an alarm so that you can wake up in time!

Food is important. If you are hungry during the test, you will not be able to focus well. Do not eat heavy food, but do eat food that will give you energy. Being nervous is natural before a test, but it is not good to be too nervous. If you start to panic, take some time to relax before you continue.

You must understand the test. Look through the test to give yourself an overall picture. Also, read the directions so that you know exactly what you have to do. Finally, make sure to keep an eye on the time. Too slow and you might not finish. If you finish early, then you can go back and check.

Try this

After reading the text above, close your textbook and in 30 seconds summarize the content to your partner. You can use Japanese or English.

Transcript Completion

Watch the news clip.

AZUZ: And that is one thing I do not miss about school: the tests. We will be thinking about you high school students this Saturday, January 26, because we know a lot of you are gearing up for a big one — the SAT. Regardless of whether you're stressing out over that or if you are concerned about any standardized testing in any grade, check this out. CNN Student News has you covered with some tips.

AZUZ: There's not much that's fun about taking a test. But there are some things that can make the process less painful. So to start, make sure you sleep. Not during the test. Most experts recommend getting eight hours the night before the test, but if you're cramming and that's not possible, get at least a few hours, so you're awake enough to focus on the questions and not on how tired you are. Also, you should set an alarm, and a backup alarm, and check that both have the right a.m., p.m. setting. Don't ask me how I know.

Next, eat. Not during the test. Grab a meal or a healthy snack before test time. It will give you energy and help you focus on the questions and not on how hungry you are. The trick here is, you want something light and energizing like cereal or fruit, but not something heavy like pizza. That can make you sleepy. Third, breathe. Being nervous is natural and can actually help you focus, but don't get so wound up that you're turning blue and sweating all over the scantron. Take some deep breaths, shut your eyes for a moment, if you have to. Try to stay positive and focus on each question.

So, keep calm and follow directions. That's tip four. It's a good idea to grance over the entire test first thing, so you know what's coming. And carefully read up on what's being asked of you. That will prevent a lot of stupid mistakes. And finally, keep the pace. If your test is 10 questions, don't spend half of your time on the first one. Stumped? Answer what you know and come back later. Finish early? Take the extra time to go over your answers and make sure they're in the right places. Being first to turn it in won't help your grade, but acing it can help you make the grade.

CNN Student News – 2012

Comprehension Questions

Mark the following sentences True (T) or False (F). Underline the key words or phrases in the transcript which support your answer.

Paragraph 1

[T / F] (1) Azuz liked tests at school.
[T / F] (2) This report will help people who are worried about testing.

Paragraph 2

[T / F] (3) This advice will make taking a test fun.
[T / F] (4) It's better to sleep for a few hours than for eight hours.

Paragraph 3

[T / F] (5) Being nervous can have a positive effect on test-taking.
[T / F] (6) If you are too nervous, you might try closing your eyes.

Paragraph 4

[T / F] (7) Reading the instructions will help you to not make mistakes.
[T / F] (8) Handing in your paper early will help you get a high score.

Notes:

gear up for: ～に対して準備する / **the SAT:** 米大学進学適正試験 / **stress out over:** ～にイライラする / **in any grade:** どの学年であっても / **backup:** 予備の / **grab a meal:** 素早く食べる / **energizing:** 栄養を与える / **get wound up:** ～にこだわる / **turn blue:** 真っ青になる / **scantron:** マークシート / **read up on:** 読み込む / **make the grade:** 合格する

Writing I

Select the best choice to complete the sentence.

1. I didn't want to (　　　　) in the thick factory smoke.

   a. breathe　**b.** breathes　**c.** breathed　**d.** breathing

2. I was (　　　　) by the difficult question from my student.

   a. stump　**b.** stumps　**c.** stumping　**d.** stumped

Writing II

Select the best choice to complete the sentence.

1. Thanks to your (　　　　), I was able to solve my computer's memory problem.

2. I am going to (　　　　) all night for the midterm test.

   tip / glance / cram / standardize / ace

Writing III

Write a summary of the news using the four words which are the correct answers to Writing I and Writing II above. Underline each of the four words.

12

Unit 4

Soccer Brain Study

Reading

This is an introduction to the news.

There have been many studies about head injuries in football. People are worried that repeated impact to the head can cause damage to players' brains. Scientists have shown that there is a problem in football. When players take a lot of hits to the head their brains can swell, which can lead to loss of memory and the ability to think well.

Until recently, there has not been much research about heading the ball in soccer. There is a fear that this activity may also cause damage to the brain. The clip today is about a new study on head injuries in soccer. Although the study is small, there is evidence that if you head the ball too much then you might damage your brain. The study looks at how water molecules move through players' brains. If the brain has been damaged, the molecules move differently. The study seems to show that heading the ball too much can cause injury to the brain.

The CNN medical correspondent says that the two sports are similar in that when a player is hit in football or heads the ball in soccer, their brain moves inside the skull in a similar way, and this is what causes damage to the brain.

Try this

After reading the text above, close your textbook and in 30 seconds summarize the content to your partner. You can use Japanese or English.

Transcript Completion

Watch the news clip.

AZUZ: Well, there's a new study out about head injuries in sports. You might be thinking football. This one is about soccer. It was just a small study, just 39 players, so the results will need to be seen in other players before they can be considered conclusive.

The research says players who hit the ball with their heads too much could cause damage to their brains. The study looked at how water molecules move through the white matter in the players' brains. In healthy brains, there's a solid pattern. In injured brains, the molecules move more randomly.

So how many headers is too many? Well, the study says if you take more than around 1,300 headers per year, that's when you could be causing some damage. The effect is similar to head injuries in football. You can see it on this animation. When the head is hit, the brain swells up. In the soccer study, scientists said the damage seemed to be connected with memory problems and how quickly players' brains could process information. Dr. Sanjay Gupta says the sport isn't what matters here. The big issue is how the brain is affected.

DR. SANJAY GUPTA, CNN MEDICAL CORRESPONDENT: Keep in mind, a lot of the focus has been on football specifically, and we've done a lot of reporting on this. But the thing to keep in mind is, when you think of the brain, it's the brain movement within the skull that's the bigger issue, even more so really than the brute force sort of these impacts. So it's how the brain reacts to the — to the force.

CNN Student News – 2011

Comprehension Questions

Mark the following sentences True (T) or False (F). Underline the key words or phrases in the transcript which support your answer.

Paragraph 1

[T / F] (1) The study is about a positive effect of sports.
[T / F] (2) Football is the main sport considered in the study.

Paragraph 2

[T / F] (3) Heading soccer balls is dangerous.
[T / F] (4) The study examines water molecules moving all over the brain.

Paragraph 3

[T / F] (5) Less than 1,300 headers per year is OK.
[T / F] (6) The brain gets bigger when it is hit.

Paragraph 4

[T / F] (7) There has been a lot of reporting about soccer.
[T / F] (8) The movement of the brain is the most important issue.

Notes:

consider: 考える / **white matter:** (脳の) 白質 / **randomly:** ふぞろいに / **header:** ヘディング / **effect:** 効果 / **be similar to:** 〜に似ている / **swell up:** 腫れ上がる / **be connected with:** 〜と関係がある / **affect:** 〜に影響を及ぼす / **keep in mind:** 覚えておく / **specifically:** とりわけ / **skull:** 頭蓋骨 / **brute force:** 力づくの / **sort of:** 〜のような

Writing I

Select the best choice to complete the sentence.

1. The cyclist was hit by a car, but luckily his (　　　) were not serious.
   - **a.** injury **b.** injuries **c.** injured **d.** injuring

2. After the earthquake, the building structure was still (　　　).
   - **a.** solid **b.** solider **c.** solidest **d.** solidly

Writing II

Select the best choice to complete the sentence.

1. A typhoon hit my town, but the (　　　) was light.
2. It's going to take a long time to (　　　) all this data!

process / conclusive / impact / damages / molecules / issue

Writing III

Write a summary of the news using the four words which are the correct answers to Writing I and Writing II above. Underline each of the four words.

Unit 5

Google Glass for Firefighters

Reading

This is an introduction to the news.

Google Glass is a kind of eyeglasses which is also a computer. People wearing the Glass can use it to do all the usual things a computer can do, like take pictures and read mail. Google says that using the Glass can be easier than using a computer, though it is still quite expensive. They had a competition asking for suggestions for apps for this device.

A firefighter named Patrick Jackson, who already had some experience of designing apps, applied. His idea was an app for firefighters that could help them save lives. He suggested that firefighters wearing the Glass and using the firefighter app could receive fire notifications, find the nearest fire hydrants, and even see floorplans of burning buildings.

There are a few problems with the app, though. The firefighter's helmet is not the right size for the Glass to fit well, so the Glass cannot be worn when firefighters actually go into a burning building. Another problem is that nobody is sure what will happen if the Glass gets very hot. Finally, some of the functions of the app rely on both an Internet connection and a GPS signal, and those are not always available.

Try this

After reading the text above, close your textbook and in 30 seconds summarize the content to your partner. You can use Japanese or English.

Transcript Completion

Watch the news clip.

AZUZ: It's possible that Google Glass could be added to that list. It's a type of computer that users can wear like eyeglasses. It can be used to get directions, take pictures, see text messages, and potentially help people working in dangerous conditions communicate. But it has its limitations, and the $2,000 price just scratches the surface.

ZAIN ASHER, CNN CORRESPONDENT: Google says Glass can make reading emails easier. It can also help you navigate in an unfamiliar city. But can it save lives? 34-year-old firefighter Patrick Jackson thinks so. He wants firefighters to use Google Glass to receive notifications on fires in their area and to help find people trapped inside burning buildings.
PATRICK JACKSON, FIREFIGHTER: OK. Glass. Show floor plan.
ASHER: And to help rescue passengers in burning vehicle. He's also developed a way for Google Glass to use GPS signals to search for the nearest fire hydrants.
JACKSON: OK, Glass. Find a hydrant. Two hundred feet north.

ASHER: Jackson, who is based in North Carolina, was one of 8,000 people selected to develop apps for Glass last year in Google's "If I had a Glass Challenge". 150,000 people applied. His suggestion on how firefighters could use Glass to save lives caught Google's attention. Google gave him some guidance on writing an app for firefighters. But since Jackson already had experience in computer engineering and had written android apps in the past, he didn't need much help.

Jackson says he's still trying to iron out a few minor details. For example, Glass still doesn't fit well inside a firefighter's mask. So firefighters have only used it on their way to a fire, and not inside an actual burning building. There are also some questions about what would happen if Glass actually got close to a real blaze. Would they melt, for example? Also, its reliability in finding fire hydrants or receiving fire alerts depends on Internet connection and a reliable GPS signal. So, certainly still a few kinks to work out. Zain Asher, CNN, New York.

CNN Student News – 2014

Comprehension Questions

Mark the following sentences True (T) or False (F). Underline the key words or phrases in the transcript which support your answer.

Paragraph 1

[T / F]   (1)   Google Glass is a computer with various functions.
[T / F]   (2)   Google Glass seems to be a perfect tool.

Paragraph 2

[T / F]   (3)   Google Glass could inform firefighters when there is a fire.
[T / F]   (4)   Fire hydrants cannot be found by this item.

Paragraph 3

[T / F]   (5)   150,000 people were asked to make apps for Glass.
[T / F]   (6)   Jackson needed a lot of help from Google to design the app.

Paragraph 4

[T / F]   (7)   Firefighters have already tried Glass.
[T / F]   (8)   Jackson doesn't know if Glass will melt if it gets hot.

Notes:

text message: 携帯メール / **scratch the surface:** 表面に傷がつく / **floor plan:** 見取り図 / **GPS: Global Positioning System** 衛星利用測位システム / **hydrant:** 消火栓 / **blaze** (n.): 炎 / **kink:** 支障

Writing I

Select the best choice to complete the sentence.

1. This printer has excellent (　　　). It never has printing problems.
   - a. rely   b. relying   c. reliable   d. reliability

2. The ship (　　　) carefully around the rock in the bad storm.
   - a. navigate   b. navigated   c. navigating   d. navigation

Writing II

Select the best choice to complete the sentence.

1. This apartment is (　　　) the best, because it's close to the station.
2. My younger brother likes (　　　) and their big red trucks.

   notification / firefighters / alerts / app / potentially / iron out

Writing III

Write a summary of the news using the four words which are the correct answers to Writing I and Writing II above. Underline each of the four words.

Unit 6

Women on Submarine

Reading

This is an introduction to the news.

For a long time in the U.S. Navy, women were not allowed to serve aboard submarines. Then, in 2009, the rule changed, and women were chosen for work under the water. It is a very tough job, because there is not much space or sunshine on the submarine, which must stay under the water for long periods of time.

Marquette Reid was training to be a pilot at the naval academy when the rule changed. She decided that she wanted to work on submarines. The training was long, and she did not get enough sleep, but finally she was able qualify as an officer. She received her dolphin, a device which means she has reached a high level of submarine operation. At the time this clip was made, there were only three women who had reached this level.

Now, having got married, she is Marquette Leveque, and she feels that it is a big honor to be allowed to work on the submarines. She says that she is not any different from the male sailors and believes that she will be treated the same way. Because she is an officer, perhaps one day she will be in command of a nuclear submarine during war.

Try this

After reading the text above, close your textbook and in 30 seconds summarize the content to your partner. You can use Japanese or English.

Transcript Completion

Watch the news clip.

1-48
1-52

AZUZ: Until a few years ago, you wouldn't have found a woman serving aboard a U.S. Navy submarine. It just wasn't allowed. The rule changed in 2009, and some of the first women who were chosen to do it said it wasn't tougher because they were women; it was tougher because of the training. We're going to dive a little deeper on what it's like to serve the country underwater.

1-49
1-53

CHRIS LAWRENCE, CNN CORRESPONDENT: It's a new frontier for female sailors. Submerged for months, no sun, no space, no sleep.
LT. JG MARQUETTE LEVEQUE, U.S. NAVY: Very well, dive.
LAWRENCE: Lieutenant Junior Grade Marquette Leveque is one of the first women to qualify for submarine duty.
LAWRENCE <on camera>: Was it everything you expected?
LEVEQUE: I got a lot less sleep than I imagined I would.
LAWRENCE <voice over>: We met Leveque a few years ago when she went by her maiden name, Reid.
UNIDENTIFIED FEMALE: Marquette Jay Reid.
LAWRENCE: She was a cadet at the naval academy when the Pentagon opened sub duty to women.
LEVEQUE: At the time, I was flying. I was a pilot. Selected to be a pilot after graduation.

1-50
1-54

LAWRENCE: Leveque decided her future was under the water, not soaring above it. And she wasn't afraid of breaking a barrier.
LEVEQUE: I see us being just like our male counterparts, and I think that we'll be accepted the same way.
LAWRENCE: Leveque earned her dolphin.
UNIDENTIFIED MALE: Congratulations, great job.
LAWRENCE: A gold chest device that means she's mastered submarine operations.
UNIDENTIFIED MALE: Sign the book.
LEVEQUE: Yes, sir.
UNIDENTIFIED MALE: It's been a long time coming, right?
LEVEQUE: Yeah.

1-51
1-55

LAWRENCE: It took a year of nuclear training, three more months at submarine officer school.
LEVEQUE: Dive. Make your depth two five zero feet.

LAWRENCE: And then her first sea tour.
LEVEQUE: It's a huge honor to finally really feel like I'm a part of the submarine community.
LAWRENCE: In fact, Leveque is one of only three women to qualify as unrestricted line officers. That's big, because it means down the road she would be eligible to one day assume command of a nuclear powered sub. And it's pretty clear that whenever war is waged under water, women are going to be a part of that fight.
Chris Lawrence, CNN, the Pentagon.

CNN Student News – 2012

Comprehension Questions

Mark the following sentences True (T) or False (F). Underline the key words or phrases in the transcript which support your answer.

Paragraph 1
[T / F]　(1)　Until recently, women were not allowed to work on submarines in the U.S. Navy.
[T / F]　(2)　After 2009, women were allowed to serve on submarines.

Paragraph 2
[T / F]　(3)　Submarine sailors spend a lot of time under the surface of the ocean.
[T / F]　(4)　Leveque changed her name in the last few years.

Paragraph 3
[T / F]　(5)　Leveque wanted to be a pilot more than a sailor.
[T / F]　(6)　Dolphin pins are given to those who have the skills to work on submarines.

Paragraph 4
[T / F]　(7)　Before she went to sea, Leveque had just a year of training.
[T / F]　(8)　Leveque might be in control of a submarine one day.

Notes:
dive deeper: より深く探検する / **new frontier:** 新しい領域 / **lieutenant junior grade:** 二等海尉 / **go by:** 〜の名で通っている / **maiden name:** (既婚女性の) 旧姓 / **cadet:** 士官候補生、士官学校生 / **naval academy:** 海軍兵学校 / **Pentagon:** 国防総省 / **soaring:** 舞い上がる / **counterpart:** 同等の人 / **earn:** 得る / **device:** 記章 / **it's been a long time coming:** ここまでは長い道のりだった / **sea tour:** 海上勤務 / **unrestricted line officer:** 非制限兵科 将校 / **down the road:** 将来いつか / **assume command of:** 〜の指揮を執る / **wage war:** 戦争をする

Writing I

Select the best choice to complete the sentence.

1. This train ride is (　　　) because it's so crowded.
   - a. tough　b. toughly　c. toughness　d. toughest

2. The car was so heavy that it was soon (　　　) in the river.
   - a. submerge　b. submerges　c. submerged　d. being submerged

Writing II

Select the best choice to complete the sentence.

1. She needs a high score in order to be (　　　) for the program.
2. You can (　　　) to be a teacher if you pass the exam.

   eligible / navy / duty / nuclear / submarine / qualify

Writing III

Write a summary of the news using the four words which are the correct answers to Writing I and Writing II above. Underline each of the four words.

Unit 7

iPhone Musician

Reading

This is an introduction to the news.

Curtis Fields was not a rich man. He did not have enough money for a keyboard, so he started making music using his iPhone. He thought that playing music like this was just fun, he did not think that it could result in him becoming famous.

He went to an audition and played his iPhone. A manager named Ray Daniels said he was interested in working with Curtis. Ray became Curtis's manager, and they went together to see a music producer named LA Reid, who worked at Epic Records. When Curtis played LA Reid his song, LA Reid took out his drumsticks and started tapping along with the song. Curtis was very surprised. When the song was over, LA Reid invited Curtis to join the record company.

Since then, Curtis has had the chance to play on the television and at an awards ceremony. Curtis is not yet an artist who has sold more than 10 million records, but he is a talented musician who never gave up. He wants to inspire others to think about what they were born to do, to believe that they too can achieve their dreams, whatever they are, and to never give up on them.

Try this

After reading the text above, close your textbook and in 30 seconds summarize the content to your partner. You can use Japanese or English.

Transcript Completion

Watch the news clip.

AZUZ: For 'diamond', we're talking about artists like Adele, Usher, Justin Bieber. Curtis Fields, not in the diamond category, but he's starting to make a name for himself in the music industry, especially because of the unique instrument he used for his first big audition. Victor Blackwell tells us how this musician is making the most of an app-ortunity.

VICTORY BLACKWELL, CNN CORRESPONDENT: Yes, he is actually playing the guitar on his iPhone. Curtis Fields has become one of the first musicians to land a major record deal using simply his iPhone.
CURTIS FIELDS, MUSICIAN: I started playing my iPhone, because I didn't have the money to purchase a keyboard. And I didn't really think of it as, "This is something that can take me somewhere." I just thought of it as, "This as fun."
BLACKWELL: Fields went to an audition, where he met Ray Daniels, who was immediately impressed.
RAY DANIELS, FIELDS' MANAGER: Actually, I remember Curtis calling me the next morning like, "Hey, are you serious about working with me, because my son and my girl are sleeping on the floor, my ..."

BLACKWELL: Daniels agreed to be Field's manager, along with colleague Davon Washington. They took him to meet music executive LA Reid at Epic Records.
FIELDS: I was playing this song in LA Reid's office as my audition. And he pulls out his drumsticks from under the table and starts like, tapping along in the rhythm like, and just jamming. And it was like, one of the most surreal moments ever. But after that, he was like, "You have to be here."

BLACKWELL: This may have been the first surreal moment for the young musician, but it would not be the last. He since appeared on "The View" and also performed for the BET awards among better known artists. Fields' phone may have helped him get a deal, but it's his talent and his perseverance that will take him places. And he wants to inspire others with his story.

FIELDS: When people say Curtis Fields, I want them to think about their dreams and think about things that they really want to do in life and the things that they feel like they were put here to do. And I want them to look at those things as attainable. And it's all possible; it's just about not giving up on whatever the dream is.

BLACKWELL: Victor Blackwell, CNN, Atlanta.

CNN Student News – 2013

Comprehension Questions

Mark the following sentences True (T) or False (F). Underline the key words or phrases in the transcript which support your answer.

Paragraph 1

[T / F] (1) Adele is one artist who has sold a lot of music.

[T / F] (2) The instrument that Curtis plays is not usual.

Paragraph 2

[T / F] (3) Fields got a record contract by playing his iPhone.

[T / F] (4) Fields was rich before he got the contract.

Paragraph 3

[T / F] (5) Fields and LA Reid played together at the audition.

[T / F] (6) LA Reid was not sure about Fields' music.

Paragraph 4

[T / F] (7) It is only his phone that has made Fields successful.

[T / F] (8) Fields wants others to try and achieve their dreams.

Notes:

diamond: アメリカ音楽界で売り上げ上位ランク / **Adele:** イギリスの女性シンガー / **Usher:** アメリカのR&Bシンガー / **Justin Bieber:** カナダ出身のアイドル歌手 / **make a name for oneself:** 有名になる / **app-ortunity:** app（アプリ）とopportunityを組み合わせた造語 / **land a ~ deal:** 契約を結ぶ / **something:** すごいもの（人）/ **along with:** ～と共に / **LA Reid:** Epic Recordsの会長 / **jam (v.):** 即興的に演奏する / **The View:** ABCのトーク番組 / **BET awards:** Black Entertainment Televison賞

Writing I

Select the best choice to complete the sentence.

1. If I continue studying this year, success will be (　　　).

   a. attain　b. attains　c. attainable　d. attainably

2. The secret signal was to (　　　) on the door four times.

   a. tap　b. taps　c. tapping　d. tapped

Writing II

Select the best choice to complete the sentence.

1. The movie she watched yesterday was (　　　).

2. He plays the piano and guitar, but he wants to learn another (　　　).

   perseverance / instrument / deal / colleagues / surreal

Writing III

Write a summary of the news using the four words which are the correct answers to Writing I and Writing II above. Underline each of the four words.

Unit 8

Bringing People Back to Baseball

Reading

This is an introduction to the news.

In the U.S., major league baseball games are very popular, and often tickets sell out completely. In Japan, however, baseball games are not so popular, especially for teams that don't win much. Yokohama Bay Stars is one of these teams. Their stadium is normally only about half-full, and they need to do something to get more people to attend the games.

Jun Ikeda is the president of the Bay Stars, a team which has been at the bottom of the league for four years. His previous work was with selling products, and his task now is to get people to come to games. He wants to try and get different kinds of people to come and watch, and he is going to try some new ideas.

One of his ideas is to give a cheaper ticket price to people who have a home loan. Another idea is to give people a refund if they are not happy with the way the team played. This money can be claimed even if the team wins! A third idea is to have pro wrestling at the stadium. The president thinks, however, that the best solution is for the team to be more successful.

Try this

After reading the text above, close your textbook and in 30 seconds summarize the content to your partner. You can use Japanese or English.

Transcript Completion

Watch the news clip.

AZUZ: All right, so in the majors they are probably used to playing in front of sellout crowds or near sellout crowds, but back in their home country, some Japanese teams are struggling with half-empty stadiums. So how do you get people to come out and fill the seats and to root, root, root for the home team? Well, the Yokohama Bay Stars have some unique ideas. Alex Zolbert steps up to the plate with details.

ALEX ZOLBERT, CNN ANCHOR: It is arguably Japan's most popular sport, a national pastime. And this is the league's least successful team this year. In fact, the Bay Stars, who hail from Yokohama just south of Tokyo, have sat in the league's basement for the past four years, which helps explain all the empty seats at one of their final home games this season.

But the team has been testing some clever ideas to try to change that. But in a tough Japanese economy, how about discounts for fans who are trying to pay off their mortgage? Or offering refunds if you weren't satisfied with the team's performance? A few fans lined up after a game even though the Bay Stars won. Some of the gimmicks are the idea of team president, Jun Ikeda, a 36-year-old with a background in advertising and marketing. He tells me, it's all an effort to entice folks who aren't diehard baseball fans. How about a sideshow of pro-wrestling?

This stadium holds about 30,000 people. The average attendance this year was just over half of that. And while the boss recognizes the gimmicks might help, what will help the most is to win more games.
Alex Zolbert, CNN, Yokohama, Japan.

CNN Student News – 2012

Comprehension Questions

Mark the following sentences True (T) or False (F). Underline the key words or phrases in the transcript which support your answer.

Paragraph 1

[T / F] (1) In Japan, baseball is not popular any more.
[T / F] (2) The Yokohama Bay Stars are thinking about how to get more fans to attend games.

Paragraph 2

[T / F] (3) In the season of this report, the Bay Stars were not a strong team.
[T / F] (4) Before this year, the Bay Stars were a strong team.

Paragraph 3

[T / F] (5) Even when the Bay Stars won, you could get your money back.
[T / F] (6) The team president is trying to get more people who love baseball to attend.

Paragraph 4

[T / F] (7) The president thinks that his ideas will help improve attendance.
[T / F] (8) Winning games will improve attendance more than the president's ideas.

Notes:

sell-out crowd: 満員の観客 / **come out:** 出てくる / **step up to the plate:** マウンドに立つ / **arguably:** ほぼ間違いなく / **hail from~ :** ～を本拠地とする / **basement:** 最下位 / **tough:** 厳しい / **pay off:** 完済する / **mortgage:** 住宅ローン / **background:** 経歴 / **advertising:** 宣伝 / **entice:** 気を引く / **diehard fan:** 熱烈なファン / **sideshow:** 余興

Writing I

Select the best choice to complete the sentence.

1. In spite of bad weather, the conference (   ) was not bad.

   a. attend   **b.** attended   **c.** attending   **d.** attendance

2. He (   ) for years to win a gold medal in the Olympic games.

   a. struggle   **b.** struggling   **c.** struggled   **d.** have struggled

Writing II

Select the best choice to complete the sentence.

1. A lot of (   ) go to the early-morning market on Sunday.

2. Please bring your receipt if you want to receive a (   ).

   refund / pastime / root for / sell-out / folks

Writing III

Write a summary of the news using the four words which are the correct answers to Writing I and Writing II above. Underline each of the four words.

Unit 9

Smell of Success

Reading

This is an introduction to the news.

When we taste food, our sense of smell is very important. That is why Net Cost Market has installed artificial scent machines in their grocery stores to try and increase sales of food. These machines pump different smells into different sections of the shop to try and get people to buy more products.

A CNN producer is led through the shop without being able to see, and we can hear from her that she can smell the different parts of the shop and also hear her positive reaction to the smells. Customers have noticed the change and comment on the new scents in the different parts of the shop, and how it makes them want to buy more because everything smells so good.

The company has seen an increase of 5 percent in their sales as a result of putting these machines into the store. They are going to put more of the machines into other shops in other cities. They believe that if they make the customers hungry by using the smell machines, customers will buy more and this is not only good for the customer, but also the company which owns the shop.

Try this

After reading the text above, close your textbook and in 30 seconds summarize the content to your partner. You can use Japanese or English.

Transcript Completion

Watch the news clip.

AZUZ: One food company is hoping to sniff out higher sales by installing advertising in grocery stores that appeal to your olfactory senses. Felicia Taylor "nose" what we're talking about. She's at one of the markets that uses this technology, and she has this report on whether or not the idea of marketing to your sense of smell passes the sniff test.

UNIDENTIFIED FEMALE: If you're passing the sour pickles, it smells good. We buy the olives here. They're delicious.
FELICIA TAYLOR, CNN REPORTER: About 75 percent of what we sense as taste actually comes from our sense of smell. It's a pretty important detail when it comes to selling food. And the folks here at Net Cost Market have figured out a way to actually boost that scent. And here it is.
ANGELINA KHRISTICHENKO, NET COST: I don't eat a lot of products. They cannot attract me by a package. So the scent, that's why it can attract me. So that's why I brought this idea.
TAYLOR: Five machines are mounted on the walls throughout the store, and pump out artificial scents, like bread, chocolate, bacon and grapefruit.

TAYLOR: We want to test the power of the aromas. So we asked Tonya, one of our producers, if we could blindfold her and take her through the store and see what she could sense. And keep in mind, she's never been in this store. She has no idea exactly where we're going or what aisle we're in.
TONYA: Mmm.
TAYLOR: Something changed?
TONYA: Yes. Are we like in the bakery section? Dessert aisle?
TAYLOR: Desserts, yep. Absolutely.
TONYA: Yum.
TAYLOR: Yum?
TAYLOR: Customers had a similar reaction.
UNIDENTIFIED FEMALE: Yes. I do smell different, like breads smell different, like cooked foods smell different, you know, even like bakeries smell different, you know.
TAYLOR: And it's — does it make you want to buy more things?
UNIDENTIFIED FEMALE: Yes.
UNIDENTIFIED MALE: Everything is so yummy, and you want to buy everything.

TAYLOR: The company has stores in New York and Pennsylvania and already has plans to install the machines in all other stores, besides this one in Brooklyn.
KHRISTICHENKO: The goal is very simple, to increase the sales by making our customers hungry, satisfied and happy. Everybody will be happy.
TAYLOR: For the folks at Net Cost Market, they've already seen results with sales up about five percent in the last three months. And that adds up to the sweet smell of success. Felicia Taylor, CNN, New York.

CNN Student News – 2011

Comprehension Questions

Mark the following sentences True (T) or False (F). Underline the key words or phrases in the transcript which support your answer.

Paragraph 1
[T / F] (1) One business uses smell to advertise products.
[T / F] (2) This kind of advertising is only used in one shop.

Paragraph 2
[T / F] (3) The sense of smell and sense of taste are not connected.
[T / F] (4) Angelina buys food because of the package design.

Paragraph 3
[T / F] (5) The woman with the blindfold is a regular customer.
[T / F] (6) The customers can smell the different sections.

Paragraph 4
[T / F] (7) The company has installed the machines in every store.
[T / F] (8) The target is just to make people happy.

Notes:
sniff out: 嗅ぎ分ける / **advertising:** 宣伝広告 / **appeal:** 訴える / **olfactory:** 嗅覚の / **nose (knows):** 嗅ぎだす (知る) / **sour:** 酸っぱい / **pickles:** 漬物 / **detail:** 詳細 / **folks:** 人々 / **figure out:** 考え出す / **boost:** 促進する / **mount:** 装着する / **throughout:** ～の至る所に / **pump out:** 噴出する / **aroma:** 香り / **blindfold:** 目隠しをする / **keep in mind:** 心にとめる / **to have no idea:** わからない / **aisle:** 通路 / **absolutely:** 間違いなく / **reaction:** 反応 / **like (as filler):** その～（つなぎ言葉） / **to see results:** 結果がでる / **add up to:** 結局～になる / **the sweet smell of success:** 成功の甘い香り

Writing I

Select the best choice to complete the sentence.

1. Hummingbirds are (   ) to brightly colored flowers.

   a. attract   b. attracts   c. attracted   d. attracting

2. My uncle has an (   ) leg, but he jogs every day.

   a. artificial   b. artificially   c. artificialities   d. more artificial

Writing II

Select the best choice to complete the sentence.

1. We have a lot of (   ) during the Christmas season.
2. I like the (   ) of lavender.

   sense / scent / installed / customers / yummy / sniff

Writing III

Write a summary of the news using the four words which are the correct answers to Writing I and Writing II above. Underline each of the four words.

Unit 10

Octocopter

Reading

This is an introduction to the news.

Amazon is hoping to start a parcel delivery system using drones or another type of flying vehicle. After items are ordered online from Amazon, they will then be packaged, after which octocopters will pick them up and take them from the warehouses to customers' homes. The plan is for the octocopters, as they are known, to use GPS for guidance, not to have a human pilot.

The target is for the system, called Prime Air, to have orders delivered within 30 minutes. Amazon hopes to have the octocopters flying goods to people's homes within five years. There is a book company in Australia which hopes to use the system even sooner.

There are many problems with getting the Octocopter system started. The first problem is that it is not legal for vehicles without pilots to deliver items. The second problem is that the octocopters can only carry light items, which weigh up to five pounds. The third problem is that the vehicles can only deliver within 10 miles of a warehouse, which means that the system is very limited. The final problem is that the octocopters could hurt somebody if they hit them, so Amazon needs to work on a way to make the system safe.

After reading the text above, close your textbook and in 30 seconds summarize the content to your partner. You can use Japanese or English.

Transcript Completion

Watch the news clip.

AZUZ: Unless you are a pilot or maybe a bird, you'll probably love this idea. An order comes through at Amazon.com. It's boxed up in the nearby warehouse and sent rolling down a conveyer belt. Then it gets awesome. A drone or unmanned aerial vehicle picks it up and guided by GPS only—nobody is driving—flies it to your doorstep and drops it off within 30 minutes.

Then your car folds up into a suitcase you can pick up and take to work. OK, so maybe it's not quite the Jetsons, but it certainly sounds space age. Amazon hopes to be flying your order to your doorstep within five years, though an Australian book company hopes to airmail with drones next year.

But as cool as it sounds to say, Prime Air delivered by octocopters, that's what Air Amazon is called, it's got some challenges in just getting off the ground in the U.S. One, it's illegal. At least right now, the Federal Aviation Administration doesn't currently allow unmanned vehicles to make deliveries. Two, it won't work for everything. Just stuff under five pounds. So, kayaks won't fly.

Three, it would only work within 10 miles of Amazon warehouses, that's the range of the octocopters. And four, Amazon CEO says it can't be landing on people's heads. So, that's a kink to work out.
We can drone on about the practicality, legality, cost effectiveness and technology, but aside from all that, this would be great for ordering pizza.

CNN Student News – 2013

Unit 10

Octocopter

Comprehension Questions

Mark the following sentences True (T) or False (F). Underline the key words or phrases in the transcript which support your answer.

Paragraph 1
[T / F] (1) Drones box up the order in the warehouse.
[T / F] (2) These drones will deliver goods to your door faster than usual delivery.

Paragraph 2
[T / F] (3) This idea comes from a TV show.
[T / F] (4) Amazon wants to use the drones in less than five years.

Paragraph 3
[T / F] (5) Using octocopters to deliver goods is legal in the U.S.
[T / F] (6) There is a limit on the weight of items that can be carried.

Paragraph 4
[T / F] (7) Octocopters cannot deliver to places very far away.
[T / F] (8) Amazon is worried about the drones hitting people.

Notes:

box up: 〜を箱に詰める / **conveyer belt:** ベルトコンベア / **The Jetsons:** アメリカのアニメ / **get off the ground:** 離陸する / **Federal Aviation Administration:** アメリカ連邦航空局 / **kayak:** カヤック / **range:** 航続可能距離 / **CEO:** 最高経営責任者 / **drone on:** 際限なく延々と続ける / **cost effectiveness:** コストパフォーマンス / **aside from:** 〜はさておいて

Writing I

Select the best choice to complete the sentence.

1. Almost no one challenges the (　　　) of children going to school.

   a. legal   b. legally   c. legality   d. most legal

2. That empty (　　　) might be a good place for us to have a concert.

   a. warehouse   b. warehousing   c. warehoused   d. being warehoused

Writing II

Select the best choice to complete the sentence.

1. After the storm, my father went out to see if our (　　　) antenna was fine.
2. This driver's license limits you to operate only four-wheeled (　　　).

   drones / aerial / kink / vehicles / unmanned

Writing III

Write a summary of the news using the four words which are the correct answers to Writing I and Writing II above. Underline each of the four words.

Unit 11

Staying Safe Online

Reading

This is an introduction to the news.

There are a variety of things people should do to stay safe online. Some of them we know very well, like using different passwords for every account and making sure that files are all backed up. This week's clip looks at another dangerous area, when we log into unsecured Wi-Fi networks.

Jose Palieri, a co-worker of the reporter, connects to an open Wi-Fi network when he is in Central Park. He does not know that this network has been created by Caleb Huff, who is an expert on unwanted access to computers. When Jose enters the passwords for his Yahoo and Amazon accounts, Caleb can see the passwords on his cell phone. And because Jose already has a credit card registered to his Amazon account, Caleb can now use Jose's credit card to buy things.

It is very easy for Caleb to get to know and use Jose's personal information by setting up the Wi-Fi network. Caleb did all this just using his phone. Jose will not know that he has been hacked, and that Caleb has been shopping using his account, until he sees a bill. Lucky for Jose that this is not a real situation, just a simulation!

Try this

After reading the text above, close your textbook and in 30 seconds summarize the content to your partner. You can use Japanese or English.

Transcript Completion

Watch the news clip.

AZUZ: Keep different passwords for different sites. Don't link your social media and email accounts. Backup your important files offline. All of these are things that experts recommend to stay safer online, to keep personal info personal. And, if you ever log on to an unsecured Wi-Fi network, you could be letting a hacker know everything he or she needs to steal from you.

UNIDENTIFIED REPORTER: A breezy fall day in Central Park, and like many others, my colleague Jose Palieri is taking a break. He finds a convenient place to stop and browse the Internet. But he's about to fall into a cyber-trap. Caleb Huff is an expert in online intrusions, with all the skills of your typical hacker. He's created an unsecured public Wi-Fi network. Jose is our next victim. Right on cue.

JOSE: Central Park Wi-Fi. It's one of the only ones that's not locked down.
UNIDENTIFIED REPORTER: That's his first mistake, and it's a big one. Do not connect to open Wi-Fi networks. Jose checks his email …
CALEB: So, what we are seeing right here, uh, someone is logging into Yahoo.com.
UNIDENTIFIED REPORTER: … then he decides to go shopping.
JOSE: Winter is coming. Gotta get myself a new coat.
UNIDENTIFIED REPORTER: Something just popped up?
CALEB: Right. So, it looks like somebody is logging into their Amazon account. Their email address is displayed right here. Password is displayed right here.

UNIDENTIFIED REPORTER: Like so many of us, Jose is using the same password for email and Amazon. Another mistake. Now, we have all this information. Let's see how far a hacker might take it, using just my everyday cell phone.
(VOICEOVER): Cyber Joey, CNN? So, I'm in. I've gotten into our victim's Amazon account. I have the American Express card already in there? He saved it. There you go. I just made a purchase on his Amazon account.
UNIDENTIFIED REPORTER: Jose will have no idea he's been hacked until he sees his bill. Caleb now has access to his email account, his Amazon account and his credit card. For everyone involved, a walk in the park.

CNN Student News – 2014

Comprehension Questions

Mark the following sentences True (T) or False (F). Underline the key words or phrases in the transcript which support your answer.

Paragraph 1
[T / F] (1) Having one password for different sites is a bad idea.
[T / F] (2) Experts recommend backing up online.

Paragraph 2
[T / F] (3) Caleb Huff's real job is a hacker.
[T / F] (4) Jose is going to fall into Caleb's trap.

Paragraph 3
[T / F] (5) Jose can see Caleb logging into Yahoo.com.
[T / F] (6) Caleb can see Jose's password.

Paragraph 4
[T / F] (7) Jose's password is used to buy something on Amazon.
[T / F] (8) When Jose sees his credit card bill, he will not be surprised.

Notes:

breezy: そよ風の吹く / **be about to ~ :** まさに～しようとする / **right on cue:** ぴったりのタイミングで / **It's one of the only ones ~ :** =It's one of the few ones ~ / **lock down:** アクセスを制限する / **gotta:** have got toの縮約形 / **pop up:** （突然、予想外に）現れる / **American Express:** アメリカンエクスプレス（クレジットカードの名称）/ **a walk in the park:** 簡単なこと

Writing I

Select the best choice to complete the sentence.

1. He saw strange marks on his door. Had there been an (   )?
   - a. intrude   b. intruding   c. intrusion   d. intrusions

2. We were warned not to use (   ) networks to send private information.
   - a. unsecured   b. being unsecure   c. being unsecured   d. been unsecured

Writing II

Select the best choice to complete the sentence.

1. You should (   ) books in a library and search on the Internet.

2. The (   ) called the police as soon as her purse was stolen.

   browse / victim / bill / displayed / colleagues / purchases

Writing III

Write a summary of the news using the four words which are the correct answers to Writing I and Writing II above. Underline each of the four words.

Unit 12

Air Pollution in Asian Cities

Reading

This is an introduction to the news.

Hong Kong has a serious problem with pollution. This pollution is causing many more people to get sick with lung problems and even to die early. There is a high financial cost to the city because of this problem, which seems to be come mostly from the city's ships and ferries. Recently the city introduced rules to try and reduce this pollution by passing rules lowering the sulfur in the diesel used by its water transport.

Delhi has been named the most polluted city on the planet. It can be difficult to see because the air is so dirty. The main cause seems to be the large number of cars on the roads of the city. The government is trying to help by encouraging people to leave their car at home and use trains and buses instead. There is also a move to use cleaner forms of energy generation.

In the 1950s and '60s Tokyo was also polluted. For example, the Sumida River was very dirty. Japan passed a lot of laws to reduce the causes of this pollution and had much less of a pollution problem by the 1990s. Now, compared to other large cities in Asia, Tokyo usually ranks at the top end for the quality of the air.

Try this

After reading the text above, close your textbook and in 30 seconds summarize the content to your partner. You can use Japanese or English.

Transcript Completion

Watch the news clip.

AZUZ: CNN has reporters all around the world, and several recently discussed ways to combat pollution in the cities where they work. We'll start in Hong Kong.
IVAN WATSON, CNN SENIOR INTERNATIONAL CORRESPONDENT: I'm Ivan Watson in Hong Kong, where some of the city's 7 million residents are choking on the air they breathe.

Cases of chest infection and asthma have soared in recent years, and the problem has caused more than 2,600 premature deaths in 2014, according to a report by the University of Hong Kong, and cost the economy nearly 4 billion dollars. Think tank, the Civic Exchange, says 98 percent of the worst pollutants in the city's air come from commercial shipping and ferries. In July, Hong Kong introduced landmark new rules limiting the sulfur content of the diesel used by ships to half of 1 percent.

RAVI AGARWAL, CNN CORRESPONDENT: And after a nightfall of that, a typical Delhi morning often looks like this. You can barely see more than a dozen feet ahead of you. Now, trucks aren't allowed to ply these roads during the day, but cars are. And the sheer number of cars is a problem. Every day, 1,400 new cars join the 8.5 million already on the streets here. The World Health Organization has labeled India's capital the most polluted city on the planet. Policymakers are beginning to react, with New Delhi's government trying out what it's calling a car-free day. Delhiites will be encouraged to leave their cars at home and instead take public transport. One thing the government has been trying to do is boost renewable energy.

MATT RIVERS, CNN CORRESPONDENT: Tokyo is one of the largest metropolitan areas in the world, with tens of millions of people and the cars and the industry to go with it. And yet, pollution here, not a very big problem. In fact, as compared to most other large Asian cities, Tokyo consistently ranks near or at the top of most air quality lists. But it hasn't always been this way. Take the Sumida River, for example. Clean now, it was dark with pollution back during Japan's industrial booms of the '50s and the '60s. It took decades of environmental reforms before the problem was largely solved by the mid-1990s.

CNN Student News – 2015

Comprehension Questions

Mark the following sentences True (T) or False (F). Underline the key words or phrases in the transcript which support your answer.

Paragraph 1

[T / F] (1) The reporters all talked about how to reduce pollution in Hong Kong.
[T / F] (2) Air pollution is a big problem in Hong Kong.

Paragraph 2

[T / F] (3) Chest infections have caused people to die earlier than they should.
[T / F] (4) Health problems caused by pollution are not a problem for the economy.

Paragraph 3

[T / F] (5) There are no vehicles on the roads of Delhi during the day.
[T / F] (6) Delhi is trying to reduce the pollution by having car-free days.

Paragraph 4

[T / F] (7) The air quality in Tokyo is the same as in most other Asian cities.
[T / F] (8) Sixty years ago, the Sumida River was very polluted.

Notes:

combat: 立ち向かう / **choke on:** 〜で息苦しくなる / **chest infection:** 胸部感染症 / **asthma:** ぜんそく / **soar:** 急速にのびる / **the Civic Exchange:** 香港拠点の政策研究を行う民間のシンクタンク / **sulfur:** 硫黄 / **nightfall:** 夕暮れ / **ply:** 定期的に行き来する / **sheer number of:** 非常にたくさんの / **the World Health Organization:** 世界保健機構 / **label:** レッテルを貼る / **policymakers:** 政策立案者 / **Delhiites:** ニューデリーの人々 / **boost:** 促進する

Writing I

Select the best choice to complete the sentence.

1. I'm (　　　) late because I'm a slow walker.
   - a. consistent   b. consistently   c. consist   d. consists

2. He is living in Kobe, but he is actually a (　　　) of Tsu.
   - a. resident   b. residents   c. residency   d. residencies

Writing II

Select the best choice to complete the sentence.

1. Our (　　　) business is centered on smartphones.
2. The noise (　　　) here is caused by motorcycles.

capital / landmark / commercial / pollution / premature

Writing III

Write a summary of the news using the four words which are the correct answers to Writing I and Writing II above. Underline each of the four words.

Unit 13

Protecting Michelangelo's Paintings

Reading

This is an introduction to the news.

Michelangelo painted his fresco on the ceiling of the Sistine Chapel in 1512. The paining shows scenes from the Bible and is widely thought of as a masterpiece of the Renaissance era. It has been restored just once, but it still has very clear and strong colors. Though time is one problem for the painting, there are other factors which cause damage to it, and so new systems have been introduced to keep the painting in a good condition for the future.

There is a purification system which cleans the air and a lighting system which now uses LED lights so that there is no heat damage to the monument. As well as helping to preserve the colors, this new lighting allows the detail of the painting to be seen very clearly, which makes the people who care for the masterpiece very happy. There are sensors and cameras on the walls which count the number of people in the chapel, so that the air quality and temperature can be controlled. The Vatican is so worried about the large number of visitors that in the future they may need to limit how many people can enter the chapel.

Try this

After reading the text above, close your textbook and in 30 seconds summarize the content to your partner. You can use Japanese or English.

Transcript Completion

Watch the news clip.

AZUZ: Michelangelo's incredible achievement has been incredibly enduring. Not only for its timeless depictions of scenes from the Bible, but that it stayed in place and stayed vivid since 1512. It was restored once, from the 1980s to the 1990s, and it's seeing some enlightening changes now, because age alone isn't the only threat to the Renaissance monument.

ISA SOARES, CNN CORRESPONDENT: High above the altar in the Vatican Sistine Chapel, Michelangelo's masterpiece fresco is being seen in a whole new light. The new glow is a result of a high tech makeover, which includes a new air purification system and 7.000 LED lights, all of which will serve to illuminate, but will not cause any heat damage. 450 years after Michelangelo's death, this is an emotional moment for many.

ANTONIO PAOLUCCI, HEAD OF THE VATICAN MUSEUMS (through translator): I felt very moved and very happy, too. Why? Because I got to see the Sistine Chapel like I had never seen it before. This light allows you to see every little detail of the paintings and at the same time, it allows you to grasp and experience the Sistine Chapel as a whole, in its entirety.

SOARES: Experts hope the facelift will safeguard Michelangelo's centuries old art work from the damage caused by the ever- growing crowds, who bring in with them their dust and sweat, and breathe out carbon dioxide. So, from now on, sensors and cameras mounted on the wall will count the number of people in the Chapel and regulate the temperature and humidity. And if the numbers of tourists continue to rise, the Vatican says it may have to limit the numbers of visitors.

PAOLUCCI: No, when we reach 6 million, enough. No more. We will not exceed that number. It is the maximum number. After that, regulating the reservations, we will make sure that number is not exceeded.

SOARES: Bold and enlightening moves that will ensure that no fresco is left in the shadows. Isa Soares, CNN, London.

CNN Student News – 2014

Unit 13

Comprehension Questions

Mark the following sentences True (T) or False (F). Underline the key words or phrases in the transcript which support your answer.

Paragraph 1

[T / F] (1) Michelangelo's work was painted over 500 years ago.
[T / F] (2) The work has never been restored.

Paragraph 2

[T / F] (3) The changes in the Sistine Chapel mean the air will be cleaner.
[T / F] (4) Heat from the lights will be a problem after the makeover.

Paragraph 3

[T / F] (5) Mr. Paolucci has positive feelings about the changes.
[T / F] (6) It was the first time for Mr. Paolucci to see the Sistine Chapel.

Paragraph 4

[T / F] (7) The sensors and cameras will reduce the damage to the painting.
[T / F] (8) The Vatican has no plan to limit the number of people who can enter the Chapel.

Notes:

Michelangelo: ミケランジェロ（イタリアルネサンス期の彫刻家、画家、建築家）/ **incredible achievement:** 偉業 / **restore:** 修復する / **Renaissance:** ルネサンス（14世紀にイタリアで始まった文化復興運動）/ **altar:** 祭壇 / **Vatican Sistine Chapel:** バチカン市のシスティーナ礼拝堂 / **fresco:** フレスコ画 / **glow:** 光 / **makeover:** 改造 / **air purification:** 空気清浄 / **as a whole:** 全体として / **in its entirety:** そっくりそのまま / **facelift:** 改装 / **carbon dioxide:** 二酸化炭素 / **regulate:** 一定に保つ / **bold:** 大胆に

Writing I

Select the best choice to complete the sentence.

1. The lights brightly (　　　　) the hallway inside the dark building.
   - **a.** illuminates **b.** illuminated **c.** has illuminated **d.** has been illuminated

2. My grandmother's smile remains an (　　　　) memory for me.
   - **a.** endure **b.** endured **c.** enduring **d.** endurance

Writing II

Select the best choice to complete the sentence.

1. I liked the (　　　　) of Michael Jackson on the T-shirt.
2. The ancient pyramids of Egypt remain a builder's (　　　　).

exceeds / vivid / grasp / enlightening / depiction / masterpiece

Writing III

Write a summary of the news using the four words which are the correct answers to Writing I and Writing II above. Underline each of the four words.

Unit 14

Choosing Jury

Reading

This is an introduction to the news.

It is written in the U.S. Constitution that jurys shall be used in the trials for all crimes. Whilst judges are professional officers of the court, jurors are normal people chosen at random for duty. People are chosen to be on a jury and then asked to come to the courthouse on a specific day. Unfortunately, many of them do not come.

More jurors than are necessary are summoned to the trial. There is then a process where jurors are selected by the judge and the attorneys. This is to try and make sure that trials are fair, but actually only the judge wants a fair trial. Judges want to know if the jurors will be biased in their judgment. Attorneys on the other hand want a jury that will give them the decision that they want.

A fixed number of peremptory challenges are used by the attorneys to dismiss jurors they do not want in the jury. They do not need to explain why they are using a challenge, but if the attorneys on the other side think this because of the juror's race then the challenge may not be accepted. It is difficult for the attorneys to decide which jurors will help their case.

After reading the text above, close your textbook and in 30 seconds summarize the content to your partner. You can use Japanese or English.

Transcript Completion

Watch the news clip.

AZUZ: Article Three of the U.S. Constitution discusses the judicial power of the U.S. Section One says judges shall hold their offices during 'good behavior'. Interesting tidbit there. As far as the jury goes, Section Two says the trial of all crimes shall be by jury, and shall be held in the state where the alleged crime was committed. But how is a jury chosen?

DANNY CEVALLOS, CNN LEGAL ANALYST: The idea behind jury selection is to seat a fair and impartial jury. The reality is, that's only the judge's goal. What most people won't tell you is that the different attorneys, they want to seat the most biased jury they can possibly find ... biased towards their case. First, the court actually has to summon jurors to the courthouse. That sounds simple, but believe me, it isn't. In a typical capital case, if a court summons, say, 300 potential jurors, they are lucky if 100 show up.

And for the most part, the judge's main inquiry is ... based on, whatever your preconceived ideas are or what you've heard about this high-profile case, can you put all that aside ... and render an impartial verdict? Now, the attorneys are certainly involved. They can challenge jurors, either for cause, or using what are called peremptory challenges. This is a challenge that an attorney can use to strike a juror for any reason at all, but ... they only get a few of them, so they have to use them wisely.

An interesting point about peremptory challenges: a lawyer can use them to get rid of a potential juror for any reason, and he doesn't have to explain why. Unless the other side thinks ... he's using it to get rid of specific races of jurors. Everybody's got a theory on what race or gender thinks this way, what particular religion thinks another way, whether rich or poor people think one way or the other. And ultimately, it's all guesswork.

CNN Student News – 2015

Comprehension Questions

Mark the following sentences True (T) or False (F). Underline the key words or phrases in the transcript which support your answer.

Paragraph 1

[T / F]   (1) Juries and judges are discussed in the U.S. Constitution.

[T / F]   (2) Section Two states that trials can be held anywhere.

Paragraph 2

[T / F]   (3) The judges want a biased jury.

[T / F]   (4) The attorneys want a biased jury.

Paragraph 3

[T / F]   (5) The judges only accept jurors who don't know about the case.

[T / F]   (6) The jury can be challenged many times by the attorneys.

Paragraph 4

[T / F]   (7) Attorneys don't always explain why they are getting rid of a juror.

[T / F]   (8) It's easy to know the bias of a juror based on their race or religion.

Notes:

hold an office: 在職する / **during good behavior:** 罪過のない限り / **tidbit:** ちょっとした情報 / **alleged:** 容疑がかけられた / **seat:** 席に就く / **impartial:** 公平な / **capital case:** 死刑裁判 / **potential juror:** 陪審員候補者 / **inquiry:** 尋問 / **high profile case:** 注目を集めている裁判 / **put aside:** 〜を差し置く / **render:** 〜を言い渡す / **challenge:** 異議申し立てする / **for cause:** 正当な理由による / **strike:** 排除する / **peremptory challenge:** 専断的忌避 / **theory:** 持論

Writing I

Select the best choice to complete the sentence.

1. A fair (　　　) system is needed to remove unfair laws.
   - **a.** judicial **b.** judicially **c.** judges **d.** judged

2. I was unhappy that my boss was (　　　) against my coworker.
   - **a.** bias **b.** biases **c.** biasing **d.** biased

Writing II

Select the best choice to complete the sentence.

1. In the U.S., people often hire an (　　　) to fix their problems.
2. The (　　　) was held in the main court of the city.

   junior / trial / verdict / jury / attorney / summoned

Writing III

Write a summary of the news using the four words which are the correct answers to Writing I and Writing II above. Underline each of the four words.

Unit 15

Light Pollution

Reading

This is an introduction to the news.

There is a lot of pollution in cities around the world. We all know about the problems of bad air and noise, but today's clip looks at another kind of pollution; light pollution. Cities like New York and Las Vegas are famous for their neon lights, but there are problems with having such bright cities. One of the problems is that people are disturbed by the bright lights. For example, they may not be able to sleep well because of the light pollution. Another problem with the bright lights is that it is a waste of electricity.

Some people say that the lights can make a city more popular, attracting many tourists to a city, or that the lights can reduce crime, but in Hong Kong the leaders are planning to do something about this kind of pollution. They are going to have to make rules to limit the amount of light that is produced. This may mean that there will be a maximum brightness of lights being used, and people may have to check that this limit is being kept. If this is done, then people should be able to live their lives without lights being a problem.

Try this

After reading the text above, close your textbook and in 30 seconds summarize the content to your partner. You can use Japanese or English.

Transcript Completion

Watch the news clip.

LANCE: Next up, the bright lights of the big city — you might have seen the neon displays in New York or maybe even Las Vegas, but in this case, we're talking about Hong Kong. Now some residents say all that light from businesses and advertisements can boost a city's image or even make the streets safer. But not everyone thinks brighter is better. Richard Quest has this illuminating report.

RICHARD QUEST, HOST, QUEST MEANS BUSINESS: There are lights, bigger lights and then there's Hong Kong. The world's big cities offer culture, convenience and a cosmopolitan way of life. Living in a city, especially like this, can be anything but easy. Property prices are some of the highest in the world. The city's battle with air pollution is well known. With so much development, there's also the noise pollution. Now an entirely different problem — it's trying to live in a city of lights, lots of lights.

QUEST: Bustling with business in the heart of Hong Kong, night becomes day when the lights get switched on. This is about as bad as it gets. And remember, there are people living up there, trying to sleep, if they can.
QUEST: Professor Henry Chung has been studying light pollution for more than a decade, and says not only is excessive light a real nuisance, it's a waste of energy.
QUEST: So what would you do? Would you switch them all off?
HENRY CHUNG, CITY UNIVERSITY OF HONG KONG: It is a good idea. But, of course, we have to strike a balance. That's why I think the government has to do something. The legislation tried to control the maximum brightness produced by all these lights and check the brightness around the area. That is the best way to control light pollution.

QUEST: Well, there's been debate. There's currently no regulations in place to curb light pollution. While the city's glistening skyline's been a draw for tourists for years, now even Hong Kong's chief executive recognizes action needs to be taken.

DONALD TSANG, HONG KONG CHIEF EXECUTIVE: We realize that we have to do something about it. You look at the commercial areas, it's really bright. I think it become offensive at times, and we are now introducing virtually regulation restriction to make sure people do have a quiet night and not be disturbed too brightly in lights.

CNN Student News – 2012

Comprehension Questions

Mark the following sentences True (T) or False (F). Underline the key words or phrases in the transcript which support your answer.

Paragraph 1

[T / F] (1) Both Las Vegas and New York have bright lights..
[T / F] (2) All people think the lights are a problem.

Paragraph 2

[T / F] (3) In some ways, big cities are good to live in.
[T / F] (4) It's easy to buy a home in Hong Kong.

Paragraph 3

[T / F] (5) People live in Hong Kong's commercial districts.
[T / F] (6) Prof. Chung thinks they have to turn off all the lights.

Paragraph 4

[T / F] (7) The lights are not popular with tourists.
[T / F] (8) The government already successfully restricts light pollution.

Notes:

resident: 住民 / **boost:** 増加させる / **illuminating:** 明るくする / **cosmopolitan:** 国際色のある / **anything but:** 決して〜ではない / **property:** 資産 / **development:** 発展 / **entirely:** 完全に / **bustle:** にぎわう / **decade:** 10年 / **nuisance:** 害 / **strike a balance:** 釣り合いをとる / **legislation:** 法律 / **maximum:** 最大の / **currently:** 目下 / **curb:** 抑制する / **glisten:** キラキラ輝く / **skyline:** 空を背景とした輪郭 / **draw:** 呼び物 / **chief executive:** 長 / **recognize:** 認識する / **offensive:** 不快な / **virtually:** 事実上 / **disturb:** 邪魔する

Writing I

Select the best choice to complete the sentence.

1. We were surprised at the (　　　) of the stars away from the city.

   a. bright　b. brighten　c. brightly　d. brightness

2. Five dollars for a cup of coffee! That is (　　　)!

   a. excess　b. excessive　c. excessively　d. excessivenesses

Writing II

Select the best choice to complete the sentence.

1. Do they want to turn the park into a (　　　) zone?

2. (　　　) is one negative effect of modern living.

   restrictions / wastes / regulations / commercial / especially / pollution

Writing III

Write a summary of the news using the four words which are the correct answers to Writing I and Writing II above. Underline each of the four words.

CNN Student Newsで学ぶ読解と作文演習

©2019 年 1 月 31 日　初版発行

| 検印省略 |

編著者	関戸　冬彦
	Jake Arnold
	Ken Ikeda
	小暮　正人

発行者　　　　　原　雅久
発行所　　　　株式会社 朝日出版社
〒101-0065 東京都千代田区西神田 3-3-5
電話　東京　(03) 3239-0271
FAX　東京　(03) 3239-0479
E-mail: text-e@asahipress.com
振替口座　00140-2-46008
http://www.asahipress.com/
組版・メディアアート／製版・錦明印刷

乱丁・落丁本はお取り替えいたします。
ISBN 978-4-255-15634-7

最高クオリティの問題と解説により
圧倒的な効率でスコアUP!

韓国TOEIC運営企業YBM社が30年間のノウハウで頻出形式を徹底的に分析!

YBM TOEIC 研究所=著　　各本体3,400円+税　B5判変型

韓国TOEIC運営企業の究極の模試×10回分

TOEIC® L&Rテスト YBM超実戦模試 リスニング 1000問

TOEIC® L&Rテスト YBM超実戦模試 リーディング 1000問

リスニング
460ページ（本冊168頁、別冊292頁）

MP3音声CD-ROM+3パターンの音声ダウンロード付き

▶付属CD-ROMに通常音声を収録。
▶ダウンロードでは通常音声のほか
〈1.2倍速音声〉
〈本番環境に近い雑音入り音声〉
も提供。

リーディング
528ページ（本冊336頁、別冊192頁）

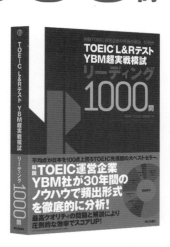

朝日出版社　〒101-0065 東京都千代田区西神田 3-3-5　TEL 03-3263-3321

生きた英語でリスニング！

CNN ニュース・リスニング
2018［秋冬］

1本30秒だから、聞きやすい！

生声CD・対訳付き・A5判　本体1000円＋税

世界標準の英語ニュースがだれでも聞き取れるようになる［30秒×3回聞き］方式！

- 大坂なおみ、全米オープン優勝の快挙！
- 「ゲーム障害」をWHOが病気と認定
- レディー・ガガ、反性暴力の声を上げる…など

スティーブ・ジョブズ 伝説のスピーチ＆プレゼン

- 伝説のスタンフォード大学スピーチ
- 驚異のプレゼンでたどるジョブズの軌跡
- 伝記本の著者が明かすカリスマの素顔
- CNNが振り返るジョブズの功績

生声CD・対訳付き・A5判　本体1000円＋税

スタンフォードの「英語ができる自分」になる教室

ケリー・マクゴニガル　生声CD・対訳付き・A5判　本体1000円＋税

意識が変われば英語力はぐんぐん伸びる！英語をモノにする意志力の鍛え方、「なりたい自分」になるための戦略…など、だれも教えてくれなかった「学習のひみつ」をスタンフォード大学人気講師が解き明かす。

セレブたちの卒業式スピーチ

次世代に贈る言葉　生声CD・対訳付き・A5判　本体1200円＋税

アメリカ名門大学で語られた未来を担う者たちへのメッセージ

- ビル＆メリンダ・ゲイツ
- メリル・ストリープ［女優］
- ティム・クック［アップルCEO］
- アーノルド・シュワルツェネッガー
- イーロン・マスク［テスラモーターズCEO］

朝日出版社　〒101-0065 東京都千代田区西神田 3-3-5　TEL 03-3263-3321

時代の最先端を伝えるCNNで最新の英語をキャッチ！

ちょっと手ごわい でも効果絶大！

CNN ENGLISH EXPRESS

世界の重大事件から日常のおもしろネタ、スターや著名人のインタビューなど、CNNの多彩なニュースを生の音声とともにお届けします。さらに、充実した内容の特集や連載によって、実践的な英語力が身につきます。

表紙イメージは2018年11月号

英語力が伸びる！4つのポイント

❶ 目的別学習ガイドの充実！
「EEを買ったはいいけど、いまいち使い方がわからない」—もうそんな心配はいりません。EEでは、目的に合わせた学習モデルを提示。自分にぴったりの学習方法がきっと見つかるはず！

❷ 本気で英語力をつけるための「繰り返し学習」
「忙しいから、とりあえず聞き流すだけ…」では、本当の実力は身につきません。厳選された素材を「精聴」し、何度も聴く「繰り返し学習」によって、初めて英語力がつき、聞き取りが可能になります。「精聴」、しかる後に「多聴」が、学習の王道です。

❸ 継続学習を実現する最適な学習量
「精聴」による学習効果を最大限に得るために分量を最適化。気に入った素材を繰り返し聴くことで、リスニング力、発信力をはじめとする英語力が確実に向上し、さらに継続的な学習が可能になります。

❹ 2020年東京五輪を見据えた、充実の新連載！
NHK英語元講師・江口裕之先生の「英語で伝えるニッポン」や、マンガとゲームで日本を学んだベンジャミン・ボアズ氏のエッセイを絶賛連載中。

iPhone、iPad で読める電子版もApp Store で大好評発売中！

CNN ENGLISH EXPRESS
CNNライブ収録CD付き
毎月6日発売
定価1,240円（税込）
http://ee.asahipress.com/

朝日出版社　〒101-0065 東京都千代田区西神田 3-3-5　TEL 03-3263-3321